THE PORT
SERIES

Series Titles

Broken On the Wheel
Barbara Costas-Biggs

Sparks and Disperses
Cathleen Cohen

Holding My Selves Together: New and Selected Poems
Margaret Rozga

Lost and Found Departments
Heather Dubrow

Marginal Notes
Alfonso Brezmes

The Almost-Children
Cassondra Windwalker

Meditations of a Beast
Kristine Ong Muslim

Praise for
Barbara Costas-Biggs

Barbara Costas-Biggs, in her debut full-length collection *Broken On the Wheel*, is able to over and over again, poem after poem, use a direct intensity to illuminate the domestic, the forgotten, and the beauty that clings to people and places for longer than most realize. These poems carry so much intention and dedication with them that I found myself slowing down to meet their pace. I love the world of these poems. I know there's sugar in the jar even if we don't need sugar right now. I know there are drugs down the street, but everyone starts the block party sober. I know the river is there to carry our bodies a little while, but if we stay in too long it will drown us. This is the work of a poet that knows the name of the one species of hummingbird in Ohio, but keeps that name tucked under her tongue. This book is a whole world, one I know and keep close to me, and I can't imagine a way it could be more complete.

—Darren C. Demaree
author of *a child walks in the dark*

"Things can be idyllic and then ugly," Barbara Costas-Biggs writes. "A basket of pears in ochre, then piss the same color." The speaker of these poems is a mother, a griever, a "hope-against-hoper," so it's no wonder this collection is packed with epiphanies and memories and crapshoots—"That in-between stuff./ What we, I hope, are mostly made of." *Broken On the Wheel* is a perceptive, masterful debut.

—Maggie Smith
author of *Goldenrod* and *Good Bones*

Barbara Costas-Biggs tells us, right from the start, what to expect: "one moment can change everything" and we see the what-ifs and the second-guesses throughout the collection: the doubts about motherhood and marriage, the fears about one's body and one's nation, the deliberation and desire for a different life. *Broken On the Wheel* takes the reader on a journey through every woman's life—the yearning and hope and grief and love, which "seems like a crapshoot". These poems hold our hand as we walk with them, forcing us to remember that like the poet, we too are "built of stars. / That every flash of a firefly is a miracle."

—Courtney LeBlanc
author of *Exquisite Bloody, Beating Heart*

In her debut collection, *Broken On the Wheel*, Barbara Biggs wants to show us the world for what it really is—a place where best friends die of overdoses and the most kindness (she) sees in the world happens in the Aldi parking lot, as shoppers "pay forward," passing their carts to other shoppers, instead of returning them to the hook up mechanism and collecting their twenty-five cent investment. She is a master sarcasmist. And though there may be little love lost on humankind (other than her kids, a few family members, best friends, strays, etc.), her regard for animals, even the lowliest, is voluminous. She freely admits her memory isn't always to be trusted, and like many who are just shy of mid-life, she dips into her past, which helps us understand where some of her dubiety comes from. Biggs's honesty is intense, her attention to detail remarkable, and reader, you will love her for it.

—Kari Gunter-Seymour
Ohio Poet Laureate
author of, *A Place So Deep Inside America It Can't Be Seen*

The poems in *Broken On the Wheel* speak directly to my Gen X heart. Infused with a healthy cynicism, each poem carries you through the ordinary moments that define our lives, yet address the enormity of our mortality. Such moments can only be appreciated through the lens of a writer who deeply appreciates the presence of the absurd, as it is juxtaposed with the average, every day look at ourselves. I savored every word of this book. It felt like letters from an old friend from the 1990s.

—Amanda Page
founder of *Scioto Literary*
editor of *The Columbus Anthology*

Broken
On the Wheel

Poems by

Barbara Costas-Biggs

Cornerstone Press
Stevens Point, Wisconsin

Cornerstone Press, Stevens Point, Wisconsin 54481
Copyright © 2021 Barbara Costas-Biggs
www.uwsp.edu/cornerstone

Printed in the United States of America.

Library of Congress Control Number: 2021945100
ISBN: 978-1-7333086-9-4

Excerpt(s) from *The Unabridged Journals of Sylvia Plath* by Sylvia Plath, edited by
Karen V. Kukil, copyright © 2000 by the Estate of Sylvia Plath. Used by permission
of Anchor Books, an imprint of the Knopf Doubleday Publishing Group, a division of
Penguin Random House LLC. All rights reserved.

Cover Art: Kenyon Cox, *Lengthening Shadows*, 1888, oil on canvas, Smithsonian
American Art Museum, Gift of Mrs. Ambrose Lansing, 1983.

Cornerstone Press titles are produced in courses and internships offered by the
Department of English at the University of Wisconsin–Stevens Point.

DIRECTOR & PUBLISHER   EXECUTIVE EDITOR   SENIOR EDITORS
Dr. Ross K. Tangedal   Jeff Snowbarger   Lexie Neeley & Monica Swinick

SENIOR PRESS ASSISTANTS
Claire Hoenecke, Gavrielle McClung

PRESS STAFF
Rosie Acker, CeeJay Auman, Shelby Ballweg, Megan Bittner, Kala Buttke, Caleb Feakes,
Emma Fisher, Camila Freund, Kyra Goedken, Brett Hill, Adam King, Pachia Moua,
Annika Rice, Alexander Soukup, Bethany Webb, Maggie Weiland

*For John, and also for Jack and David,
and especially for my father, Peter Costas*

Contents

weeping of all

this orbit

Broken
On the Wheel

Why the hell are we conditioned into the smooth strawberry-and-cream Mother-Goose-world, Alice-in-Wonderland fable, only to be broken on the wheel as we grow older and become aware of ourselves as individuals with a dull responsibility in life?

—Sylvia Plath

The Doe

Upside down you are ensnared
in the barbed wire, north side
of the pasture, borderland between

garden and gully, all the thrash gone out of you.
I crouch, show you my hands.
Farmer without a gun. A hope-against-hoper that

I will never need one of those. I live with my
head in the dirt. In spring, I plant
rows of lettuce for spoiled

cattle. Extra corn for raccoons.
Do not welcome the fox to the chicken yard
though I defend her. Her kits are hungry.

I imagine your last great leap—long legs
tucked to belly. You've done it hundreds
of times. Sailed over fences, brush, downed

trees. My missteps haven't yet left me
for dead the way yours have.
A stroke of your flank, my useless

offer of comfort. At eye-level, I see
you, seeing me. One misstep is the thing
you've taught me to avoid—

how one moment can change everything.

the things we fix

Trillium as Accomplishment

with a line from Jane Kenyon

I didn't start out down the path looking
for them, but there they were:
three white petals cloaked

in the loveliest green, pollen dusting
the leaves, six stamens pointing right
up at me. It was an accident, this time

I had salvaged to take a walk.
I wish I could sketch this flower
with a pencil on thick, uneven artist's paper.

I would bring it back
to show you that I had accomplished
something: a drawing on paper

seems like something more, seems
like enough and better.
I walk home, toppling the grasses in the field.

Circa 1994

after Jason Isbell's "The Life You Chose"

It wasn't Jack and Coke, it was Southern Comfort in Taco
Bell cups full with ice, no doubt on our way to another
viewing of Pulp Fiction or to Hoover Reservoir to steam
windows and dream of big cities and rock stars and riot girls
and whatever else it was that made sense to a seventeen
year old girl whose heart was only half alive. I was always
reading The Bell Jar, listening for that old brag of my heart
but never trusting it; sure that whatever it told me to do
would be wrong.

Last night was my 20-year high school reunion. I skipped
it, not even curious about how the faces I knew all those
years ago have aged, because it wouldn't be a surprise. I know
what they had for breakfast this morning—thanks to the
phone in my hip pocket that dings and dings and keeps my
Twitter feed current. I skipped it and got drunk with people
I don't know and told them all, "I'm skipping my 20-year
reunion for this," as if that brag was meaningful. It didn't
make me feel younger.

This town I live in now doesn't leave much to the imagination.
Tucked in a valley, surrounded by rivers and foothills. Not
even outlet malls to help me waste an afternoon. I have a
house that's too small. I have children getting too big too
quickly. I drive an hour to work. On Friday mornings, if my
timing is right, I can speed alongside the Amtrak Cardinal
and wish and wish and wish and remember.

I Dream of My Father In a Greek Landscape

If you want to get to heaven
Over on the other shore...
—"Good Shepherd", arr. by Jorma Kaukonen

I dream of my father in a Greek landscape,
spit and lamb turning beside him.

He is familiar in my kitchen, his stance easy,
wine-stained teeth. I bet his hands

still smell like garlic, lemon, red onion.
All of this ground is sacred because you stand

there, and your father before stood there. Your brother,
now, too. That mountain might be Parnassus, though

maybe it's Pinnacle Peak, or this could very
well be Troon. We could be in the middle of the Sonoran.

I don't know—you won't tell me because
this is a dream, and like all good dreams, I could swear
it happened.

Discernable Proof

Our fire wouldn't catch, so you tried
carburetor cleaner, sprayed it in a straight
line at the smoldering kindling. Ignition.
Flames shot so high, I worried our
eyebrows would catch and my contacts would melt.
Our children ran around the fire like tiny wild men,
their voices rising to the treetops.
I asked if roasting marshmallows on a fire
started with carburetor cleaner was a good idea.
You replied that it was better than when I started
one with the Restoration Hardware catalog.
The cleaner burned away, you said. The poison
rose up and away, gone quickly into the canopy.
I looked for some discernable proof: glowing
leaves or falling fireflies. Nothing.

After dark, after I'd given the dog what he
needed to make it through the noise,
after we'd wiped and re-wiped charred, sticky
marshmallow remains from the children,
we walked across the road with glasses of
wine and folded camp chairs
to Mt. Zion Cemetery.
I was skeptical that we would be able to
see the fireworks from the town downriver.
I was sure that hills would
obscure our view. I was wrong.
Colors burst into the sky,
the children ran figure eights around tombstones
and I remembered why (even though quiet and rolling
and lovely), I'd always avoided the place. Your chair,
placed near a small, mossy stone. A lamb
perched on its top.

The sky silent and dark again, the smoke
rolling into the valleys,
we walked back to break the silence
in our own yard.
We put the children to bed, sat
under Orion's Belt, finishing the wine,
watching the embers of the carburetor fire
shimmer and pop, doing just fine on its own
fueled by wood from the sugar maple
we reluctantly cut in the spring.

I tick these things off in my mind:
the maple, the river, the stones, the children.
The things in the way, the things we fix
or can't fix. The proof that isn't always there.
I write this to remember that
we keep the fire burning.

I Speak to My Husband From Inside a Whale

A blue whale's tongue is heavy as an elephant.
Its tail, the wingspan of a propeller plane.
Its heart like a Volkswagen, protected by a ribcage that
I could move a sofa into, hang art, pour a beer.
My tongue sometimes gets heavy, too, uses up excuses
and fails, again and again. Your name is always
there, yet I forget you made me whole. Instead,
I tell you how you left flatware in the sink, unwashed.
Watch how I go deep underwater for days, elude
all human contact, wave nothing but that great tail,
no trace of above water breathing. Oh, secretive mammal,
largest of all, our path propels
us far into the distance, only to be called
back to the same place again and again.

Yesterday I Asked My Son

Do you see that there? The bee
stumbling into a flower, legs padded
with pollen, his hive-mate heavy-flying
to the clover of the neighbor's unmowed
yard. Yesterday, we saw a katydid on a high
electrical wire like a perfectly balanced
leaf. Yesterday, we could look at the sun,
right at it, behind the smoke rolling
in from the west, behind the almost-fall
river fog. You called it a blood moon,
correcting yourself after saying it, No,
that's the sun, and we were mesmerized,
perhaps cautious, knowing we shouldn't
look for too long. Yesterday I almost told
you that the world is mangled-up, that
sometimes, even for all the katydids balancing
on wires, it can be me that does the injuring.

Girl of God

*Or, An Honest (to God) Conversation
with David at Six Years Old*

Who is the girl of God
      The girl of God, you must mean Mary
      who gave birth to Jesus
      it was a miracle, a real story for the ages
Mary was the one that ate the pear the one
that made people evil and
      Oh, David, it was an apple and
      it didn't make people evil
So Mary is a fairy now and
      you mean angel, I think
      both winged both fleeting
And the devil, where's he, in heaven
      He was, but he questioned God so God
      threw him out
So he's here on Earth
      Some people think so but
Do you think that
      No and I don't even think there is a devil
God was in my belly once, not like
      In your belly?
Yes, but not like I was in yours
      Which was also a miracle
      and a surprise, I might add
So you're like the girl of God
      No, I'm not
Maybe you are. Like her.
And snowflakes are tiny pieces of ice,
but you already knew that, didn't you?

Naked In the Macy's Changing Room Trying to Think of Anything Other Than the Election

Before I was grown and called lovers
"lovers." Before I was a mother and called
momma. Before I considered myself anything

I had a body: smaller, tighter, in flux
and full of flaws. Yet, always mine.
At eighteen, I slept with a boy I met

my first semester away from home.
I don't think I liked him much
but he liked me and we moved in together.

His father was a Republican with state political
aspirations. I lived in Tucson, drove
an hour to Nogales to buy

birth control at a Mexican pharmacy.
No prescription, no questions, cheap.
I ate tamales from a street vendor

and brought homemade tortillas home,
stretched and cooked over a fifty-gallon drum.
My slippery mind might be confusing

parts of these memories.
I was stoned gin-drunk living
with a boy who told me, when

he first saw me naked: I wasn't sure I'd like your body.
And when I got pregnant, told him, over
coffee, I'd made an appointment

for an abortion, he walked to the bank
handed me $250. A few days later, I drove myself
to an office in an adobe strip mall.

On the table, wearing
one of his t-shirts, paint splattered,
the doctor asked me if I was an artist.

all the precautions

Laundry List

I am vacuuming.
I am Princess Leia.
I am tasting the marinara for sweetness.
I am loading the dishwasher.
Listening down the stairs for the dryer's buzz.
Pouring glasses of milk.
I am filling the dogs' dishes.
I am watching maple leaves fall.
I am picking up crayons.
I am calling the pharmacy.
Scheduling dentist appointments.
Checking my email.
Covering the tender plants.
I am ironing shirts

> (and this is a waste of time, I know,
> but tomorrow my children have school pictures,
> so I am dragging out the
> ironing board, a wedding gift—
> yes, a damn wedding gift—
> to make sure all the imperfections
> are smoothed. *Rarely* is one of my son's
> vocabulary words. *Momma rarely irons*, he says
> to the back of my bent head).

I have a Valium hidden in my wallet.
I have the maple leaves.
I have an appointment for a tattoo.
I have mustard greens to cut.
I have the sweet marinara.
I have selective hearing.
I have a new brown bottle that rattles with the cure.

I am not the Den Mother, the Room Mother or
the Mother of All Mothers.

I have lists in my head.
I will smooth out the imperfections.
The tender plants might make it.

To My Children, Fearing for Them
with a title from Wendell Berry

It's not like when you said, after waking,
that the moon was pulling on you,
pulling you away from me.
Or when you asked me if you were sad
because I had a virus when you were in my belly.
I think my love for you is the virus, a thing
in my body that moves, organ to organ,
telling it how to spend its time, what processes
to commit to, which ones to pass on or save for later,
because sometimes the only thing that matters in this wreck
of a body is that you were once inside.

David Defines Infinity

All the numbers added to all
the numbers and then you add
that again, and it's infinity.

Multiply it, multiply it again.
Count until the world goes dark.
You'll be closer.

I am the one who measures,
as best I can, my
love for you in poems.
The proof, if not always tangible,
right here on the page.

Thursday Morning, Early, With Fog

The fog is so thick I could build a set of stairs
with it. Or a room, right in the middle

of the pasture. We hear the turkeys nearby, and we quiet,
waiting for them to cut paths in the vapor and fly blindly away.

In the driveway, this newly formed nebula,
you wave your arm around, mixing the tiny droplets

into swirls and wisps. I tell you the fog is clouds,
and I'm not really sure of the science, but it sounds right

and looks right, and the things that I tell you still hold so much
weight. If we could see from above, from the top

of our small hills (mountains once tall and snowy as the Rockies),
we could jump and then bounce right back up.

But I won't jump. At least not today. I can't ever lose sight of you:
damp and in danger of being swallowed by the gray.

Safeguards

The red-tailed hawk stood.
        Its bird-hips splayed,
legs muscular like a man, a small rodent between them.

He stood and did not eat
        did not carry the meal away
and I thought about all the blame I placed

on hawks after moving here, my flock
        of hens growing smaller
one at a time—one at a time, and then one more.

As in so many instances, so many loops that run
        on repeat in my mind
I was dead wrong about the hawk

with his legs like a man's and his talons that hold tight,
        beak curved like a scythe.
It was never the hawk.

All of the precautions I took meant
        nothing. The barbed wire coiled on the
fence posts, the terrible owl decoys, the

mirrors dangling from fishing line.
        I should understand, but I always forget.
Safeguards never mean anything.

Judas

Will you or I find it in ourselves to betray her—
meaning the one who sets the kiss in motion betrays.

A clip of silver earring with lip, the kiss that saves another.
Saved being salvation—salvation in this instance keeping another

sober, out of bed, alive for maybe another thirty days.
Each day we press cold silver into cold hands, counting days,

emptying our pockets, afraid the silver will only rattle against her heart.
And by pockets what I really mean is we have emptied our hearts.

And by betray, I also mean which of us, you or me,
will give the kiss and not end up hanged? What more can it cost us?

Justin Timberlake Sings During My First Mammogram

It's not that the room is cold
or that the radiology tech singsongs to me
    Now you can breathe

as the massive machine rotates and whirs
around my naked upper body.
I don't know that I can even name what it is

other than discomfort and worry.
Since my father's death from a cancer
that wormed its way to every molecule of his body

before it was found,
a cancer that required extensive testing
to find its origin,

I am swelled with the feeling I might be next.
But I have always been prone to hypochondria.
Above the machinations of medical devices

is *Can't stop the feeling.*
My hips want to move,
like when I drive over Scherer's Hollow:

car zigzagging, my body thrown
side to side in the driver's seat.
But this is a time for stillness.
She tells me that, the radiology tech
in a voice usually reserved for small
children and puppies: *Don't move, don't move.*

Now you can breathe.

some distance

My Life as a House

The Cape Cod home we bought is unassuming
from the outside: shutterless, begging for window

boxes and maybe hollyhocks, tall and falling
onto the cracked walkway that I thought we'd tear

up for flagstone. The sandstone that flakes
and lines the nearby roadsides—I always

thought it would make a nice pathway
too, but slippery, you told me, dangerous

when carrying bags of groceries all the way up
my arm, everything in one trip. But free, I said.

Our sensibilities so different, I thought you would jump
at my suggestion of gathering the slim stone,

packing the back of the truck, building
something new. We needed something new. After a good

thaw, on the highway closest to this house,
I can see where the springs drip—

dripping down the sandstone that lines the highways,
running in rivulets, cradled by blast

marks, places someone drilled down, packed
explosives, backed away to press

a button or pull a lever, and shattered the
sandstone that lines the highways.

Have we excavated ourselves right out of this house?
Right out of these memories? In all honesty, I

don't care about the flagstone or if the sandstone
lines the highways or the path under our feet.

I've learned to care more for the rivulets, the
surprise springs that well up and come from nowhere.

Blast marks on a highway, those curved and smooth
carvings, are only smooth from a distance.

Like so many things, the closer we get, the sharper
the focus. The sharper the words.

This Cape Cod, if it ever really was unassuming, is up a holler
on a ridge off the sandstone lined highway,

burrowed, I might say, if describing or
giving directions.

Intervention for the Intervention Specialist

There is a small dive bar just over the Ohio
Indiana line where you can still smoke indoors
and feed bills into a jukebox.
This is where you choose to write

your dissertation, away from clinging
children, from dishes crusted with breakfast,
from your husband.
The St. Pauli girl flickers above your curls.

Terms like *functional behavioral assessment* and
response to intervention line the pages and you realize
that you are not a savior. The boy from your class
that you hire to mow your lawn

will always steal from your purse
while you run to the carry-out. You love them, they
slash your tires. You will never lose
that drowning feeling when you click your car

door locked in the school parking lot.
The cornfields outside hold on to the warmth
of the day. The sunset is the same color
as the draft beer sweating in front of you.

Twenty-Two Years

I didn't think to add up the miles
between our Appalachian river
town and the northern coast of Maine.
No idea how far we went, gunning
the huge American engine through
the Adirondacks and the Finger Lakes,
finally to the top of Cadillac Mountain.
We watched the sun break through
the Atlantic; I swear it almost sizzled.
We stood with the fanny-packed, the
sock-and-sandaled, to be the first to see
the sun rise over the East coast. First
all the orange, then pink, then the blue,
the blue and the sun and I shaded my
eyes against the brightness. I threw
my arms open wide, imagined embracing
the cold water, holding on tight as best
as I could, knowing that is an impossibility.
Lately, it seems that would be easier
than taking one small step closer
to you, snaking my arms where
they have been a million times over
these last twenty-two years.

Scene From a Yellow Kitchen

for Jennifer Burchett Bentley, 1976–2014

We are a study in contrast:
our bodies, our kitchen tables,
our junk drawers.
We are light and shadow,
the skin and mystery of Caravaggio.

I arrange a pile of unopened mail
into a neat stack to prove I can be
industrious and organized.
You don't fall for it.

When you lift your arm to raise a glass,
crumbs from yesterday's dinner
stick like scabs.
You brush them into a pile
and throw them in the trashcan.

Our husbands wonder what we laugh so loudly about
from our yellow refuge.
We laugh over a stack of dirty dishes.
We laugh over the hum of the refrigerator.
We laugh from the same place.

Distance Learning

Your trees were more green and full
and the moon hung just a bit lower for you,
as to always fill your window
and whiten your face, saint-like.

Under that moon, we rode the landscape
with open windows, hoping to catch
a secret word or glimpse the perfect
phrase, frozen onto a hillside.

Years passed silently and birds flew, water
breeched bulkheads, toes were stubbed and we flew
until we were separated, wind flapping
from book pages carrying us in opposite directions.

The Gulf Stream flowed, stars blinked and faded, deer were hit.
You were still looking, but I wasn't.
At least, not nearly close enough,
until my words faded: a moon eclipsed by you.

And now, after so long, we have found each other again.
After separate epiphanies on foreign postcards,
overheard conversations and lightning storms,
still, your winds are warmer, your trees more green and full.

All Dark Places

Remind me of nights we sat
on a dock, chilled,
dipping toes in water.

Remind me how we hid behind
pampas grass, pinkies intertwined,
watching a low moon rise.

Road creases matched my heartbeat
and lead me to you.
I used to meet you at the Drexel,

arriving early so I could
watch you park, watch you
looking for me.

I want to call you, ask you
to remember all this to me.
Surely, I am not confusing

you with someone else. I don't
think you were with someone else.
Remember to me the darkened paths in the

Metropark, the one near your
father's home, where we
saw a piebald deer,

its legs thin like
spindles. Its flank
shivered when it saw us,

like my neck, when you
brushed away a mosquito.
Can I do that? Call you?

My memory is stubborn, doesn't want to be
memory at all. Remember to me all my youth,
all of you. Is that too much?

Stockholm

I don't have a coat heavy enough for
the weather in Stockholm. It's where you live
now, amongst, I imagine, blondes
in snow boots, blondes in high-collared coats,
blondes and blondes and blondes.

I picture the street signs a bit rusted
at the edges, years of snowpack and salt melt.
Picture the streets empty, the men and
women quiet, huddled around fireplaces
wishing the sun might finally rise again.
All guessing, all wondering on my end.

In pictures, the city is yellow buildings,
blue sky. I don't buy it.
You could tell me that Stockholm radiates
with saved light from the summer months
when the sun goes down in winter
and I would feel pulled there. I know that.
But in the back of my mind, I would
be thinking only of pickled herring, snowshoes.

In Stockholm, which I admit, I confuse
with Copenhagen, with Oslo and Tromsø,
I don't think I'd be content.
Too much darkness, then too
much light. In all-or-nothing situations,
I always stand frozen.

Crapshoot

for Katy

In early January, your heart shattered.
We texted into the night, me soaking

in a hotel tub, you, I imagine with a bourbon
in hand, at home, back in Ohio. We'd spent

the weekend before Christmas together,
the whole of us, our coven, and when the talk

turned not just to your husband, but all
of our men, we stilled just a bit.

I thought our forties would make things
clearer. I thought some age, some distance

from the wildness of our pasts would map
a path. But no, because nothing is clear.

You have this funny habit I love that
I learned about during our weekend

in the woods. A small notebook you keep
to write words and phrases you want

to remember: insights and epiphanies, things
too good to forget. I imagine it lined

on a shelf, next to your collages, the books
you bind by hand, the books you've written.

I realized that January night in the tub was also Epiphany,
from the Greek *to reveal*, a night of manifestations.

Now transgressions are being exposed. I have a quote
to add to your book, a thought equally terrifying and mundane,

but I give it to you, for what it's worth: It seems like a crapshoot
sometimes, love. Love, it seems like a crapshoot.

Sex In Our Forties

It's when I lost my inhibition, the constant
nag of my brain and all that I'd taught
it to believe in my twenties and thirties.
When I stopped putting my body through
ritualistic tortures of diets and fasts and
green shakes. Sometimes we leave the lights
on, and maybe my wool socks too, and the Alexa
(I call her "she" and you roll your eyes) might
be recording all of it. I don't care. My arching
back doesn't care, either. I am in a precarious
place: I want it all and yet I want nothing.
It's exhausting, the things around
sex, before anything even happens: the talking and
compromise, child-rearing, work, all the rest (yet no rest).
While I can't ignore the pleasure, I also find
myself asking, *Is this worth the effort?*

weeping of all

To You, Who Sent Me Back
Across the Continental Divide

You dropped me at the foot
of Mount Lemmon. Find

the trailhead, you said. This is the only
way to learn the desert.

I told you I come from a place
of confluence. Told you of the Ohio

and the smaller river, the one that
flooded its banks, ruined a whole settlement.

Everything within me was merging, flowing
wildly, river of white caps, river of mangled

trees, all holler and creek-dipping ridges.
Faced with shadeless ironwoods

I should have kept walking, thinking East
and muddy banks, my back to the sun.

With My Father, Sherman Hospice, February 2016

There is no way to wash away
the smell of lavender
or the taste of coffee from
a tall silver urn.

No way to unhear the pump
sitting beside your bed or the
weeping of all of the waiting
others crowding the hallway.

Tomorrow I leave the home
you made that was never my home
the bed that was never mine
in the room that is mine but never was.

You have slept for three
weeks. I filled the birdfeeders
outside your room: finches and
flickers and hummingbirds

have visited, distracting me
from your thinness,
your torso in someone else's shirt,
whatever the nurse grabbed, I guess.

You're slack-jawed and rattly
but I find things to tell you:
in 1969, when you were eighteen,
astronauts heard music while traveling

the dark side of the moon. *What could
that mean?* I might say and you would
know. I tell you back in Ohio,
we only have one species

of hummingbird, so identification
is easy. Here, I can only guess.
Who will fill the feeders
after I leave the desert for home?

Leave you here? We know I can't do that.
Leave you. I have changed my plane
ticket three times already.
I have missed my son's birthday,

his first basketball game. But what
of firsts, when this won't last?

Collecting Rocks

My husband's father collects rocks. I was wading
slipping on sandstone in Turkey Creek,
my boys forging ahead of me, heads
down, pockets full, when they told me.
It's not something I would know
or should have known, just another mystery
a layer of him newly uncovered.

I lift smooth ones from the water, imagine
placing them on my own father's headstone.
When I was young, he taught me to skip
the flat ones. They skimmed the water
while we watched, away and across
like magic, and I thought they would never

sink. In June I hiked into the Great Smokies,
chose rocks for them both.
For my husband's father,
a rock with a perfect hole.
For mine, one impossibly thin, curved
like a boomerang.

Poem In Which My Body Calls Me a Bitch

My body is screaming at me: Bitch
you are 40 years old and cannot do

this to yourself anymore.
96 hours of drinking

and your father is still dead.
You're late to the drop-off

line in the morning, head
pounding with each pothole

each chirp of each damn
bird. Your synapses spin

and tumble, bottles without
notes sent out to sea.

I can't sweet talk my body.
It knows how I lie.

Through my teeth.
Like a rug.

Lies like a dog.

Music Lessons

I spent the afternoon listening to my sons
dance to *Thunder* behind the closed door of their room
and because I'm old, I kept wondering
if Imagine Dragons are a cool band. I dropped
in every 15 minutes or so, swinging hips, doing
my best Uma Thurman impression, the six year
old actually rolling his eyes at me.
Because I was considered "of advanced
maternal age" when I had my second son, I do
not fit in with the mothers at their school.
They had their children young (too young) and
my hair is gray and I dare not even try to wear the
meshy leggings they rock. They probably know
if Imagine Dragons are cool.
When I was twelve, my dad knocked the New
Kids on the Block out of me with Traffic
with Cream with Blind Faith and every other
band that Ginger Baker played in. I think
of my dad, his patience with my terrible choices
in music. I remember sitting on the floor with
him, first the A side and then the B side of John
Barleycorn Must Die, the electricity of the first
six chords of Aqualung. Now, I temper
Imagine Dragons with The Beatles. Slip
Joni Mitchell into the playlist. I'm learning
all things take time, but my younger son
asked for a Bungalow Bill cake for his last birthday.

Walking Past Abandoned Houses,
I Think of Eric

This poem wanted to start in a condemned house, so I took
a walk to show the poem this town and asked: which one?

The poem shrugged. Shattered windows rendered black,
no flicker of blue aquarium television light. Fast-food wrappers

an altar, piled on the porch. A small pink running shoe
hole worn in the sole, stuck in a chain-link fence.

Fifteen years ago, while I was drinking flat beer in a dive bar,
my friend Eric died after getting high from a transdermal

oxycodone patch. He wrote poems I will never
forget: how he found his mother dead, her fingers

gnawed to bone by rats. His glasses always broken, crooked,
taped, his cheeks and arms scabbed.

This poem can't imagine. It wasn't this house but probably
one like it, peeling clapboard,

busted plumbing. This town smells burned out
and the burning no longer comes from the foundry

or the coke plant or steel mill. We are falling in
on ourselves, shooting heroin into our veins.

These houses—empty of furniture, food, clean clothes
laughter, shampoo—are helpless, their dirty glass eyes

begging to see something other than broken smokestacks,
shoes strung on powerlines.

The ears that heard hooves on the bricks that sleep
under pavement are long gone.

There was no Narcan for Eric, and no Narcan
for wrecked Greek revivals.

Small Town Haibun

with a line from Maggie Smith

There is a murder trial happening in the courtroom next to my office. I hear details from the court reporter and the bailiff. I dry heave in the third-floor bathroom. Sometimes I think that most kindness I see in the world happens in the Aldi parking lot. Women, some I know are widows, passing their shopping carts onto the next, waving away the offered quarters, asking that they just pass it on.

A child broken, bagged,
sunk in a lake, left under
a motel bed frame

I am getting used to life in town, again: streets with sidewalks, school buses stopping at all the corners, the church bells that hand out the hours. Since moving our lives into this house on a corner, across from a limestone church, catty-corner from a giant inflatable swan doing back and forth laps in a tiny swimming pool, my sons and I have watched a fawn and its mother eat in our backyard. The doe is a large one, eyes dark and always fixed on her baby.

Trash bag, blue cooler
odor so strong the police
won't bring it inside

The fawn has slowly lost its spots, the dot-to-dot peppering its back. It comes into the yard to eat the hawthorn berries dropped from the crooked tree, comes almost to the dining room window. We throw out apple cores for him to find, but I explain to my sons that we don't want him eating from our hands. We leave the food, he finds it. We don't want him to trust us.

The world is full of
animals. Animals. So
full of animals.

Burying the Draft Mare In February

Hooves like dinner
plates, braid still trussing her mane.
You wait for a break
in the cold—a welcome warm
snap, sun veiling the pasture
but February is tricky. You find
yourself looking back in the garden
journal, *This time last year*
it was 55, but today the air spits
snow into your eyes. You start
the tractor—first the oblong hole, dug
with the backhoe, eight feet deep—
then stop to change
implements, attach the front loader
so you can move the mare, hope
she is not already frozen
to the timothy grass.

Nigel, the World's Loneliest Bird,
Dies Next to the Concrete Decoy He Loved
—Washington Post *headline, 2 February 2018*

The papers called it an unrequited love nest
when the bird fell in love with a concrete
image of itself, but female. Lured
to a rocky coast by a looped recording,
the same gannet love song playing
over and over for only him.
What did he think when he heard that?
When his wings were spread wide, flying,
lucky bird, and he landed on Mana Island.
The other birds there but stone-heavy, motionless.
What did he think about when he built
a nest that she never moved into? He migrated
and returned for years, to find her still
there, cold, her painted yellow head fading.
His love-failure, reported on by *The Guardian*,
picked up by the AP. He'll never know
that a slight change to the looped
song brought more birds.
That the unrequited love nest he built
might not stay forever eggless,
might one day be a downy home,
gannets making songs of their own.

My Father, In His Sickness

had dreams that were so vivid to him
that I almost believed when he told us
his doctors at the Mayo had come up
with a new chemo cocktail that was going
to cure him. They had visited with this
news, woken him to tell him.
Seeing the confusion on our faces
he knew he was mistaken. He knew
we hadn't left his room in days,
except when my brother went to get records
from his collection to play on the small
turntable he'd Amazon Primed to the hospice,
me to get birdseed to fill the feeders on the patio
where he never sat, my mother to cry alone
at their home.

Puttering

I can see you in the backyard, "puttering",
you'd say, with the drip system, the life-
line of the agave and mesquite, the rest
we don't know the names of yet.
My skin and my body have never felt
fieriness like the Sonoran, never felt the drought
of dry heat. My skin and body might
wither here, might take flight after sundown
in search of humidity.
Every day seemed like a record-breaking
temperature, climbing to 121 the day
I lazed down the Salt River for the first time.

Your paloverde trees died, one then another,
in spite of their photosynthetic green bark,
and you kept puttering, looking for leaks,
looking for an answer that would keep
trees alive in the desert.

So that's what I did, some 20 years later,
puttered around the Hospice, made coffee
and small talk, hurried home for a shower
when your breathing shallowed.
Eventually you learned how to keep plants
alive in a land with no water, even strawberries,
San Marzano tomatoes.

The desert didn't return the favor.

this orbit

My Dog Lifted His Leg

and pissed on the painter's finished
canvas, the housewarming gift he gave us
two or three places ago. We had crated
and uncrated that still life each time
we decided to uproot and start again.
There was the house with the catalpa
tree, leaves big as my splayed hands together
its seed pods that dangled, brown and long
like cigars. There was a yellow
house on a hill with crumbling cement
steps—there you read from long texts
and I taught myself to knit.
When did the painter fall from our
favor, I asked you. Was it when he slammed
his vodka then called us all children?
Or when he lost a game of racquetball,
a smear of sweat on his cheek, and insisted
you were cheating. Even after that, I think
you sat with him, fishing, silent for hours.
But I could be wrong. My memory isn't
always to be trusted. I think it was when,
secondhand, I heard that he said he was glad
his estranged wife had died from cervical
cancer, that she had gotten
what she deserved for leaving him.
Things can be idyllic and then ugly.
A basket of pears in ochre, then piss the same color.

Naming

There is something not quite right here.
Taking stock of the area,
it all seems to be in order.
Pillows on sofa
ottoman in front of the chair,
frames of smiling faces
and frames of faces in profile
are all hanging, not crookedly,
the spaces between them
imperfectly measured.
Light glinting in through the curtains
is full of dust—
every swish of arm,
expansion of chest irritates it.
But still,
it's not right.
Does fear have a scent
like we say it does?
Uneasiness must have one, too.
And guilt. And impending death.
Trying to name what has gone so wrong
is impossible, here in this
still, still room,

where cut flowers have lost their sweetness
and have started into a sticky, brown decay.

Whirligig

after "Wild Geese" by Mary Oliver

It's okay, I tell him,
small boy tears on the back
of my hand, now on my forehead
where I wipe dirt from the morning's
gardening away. Let me get a better
look at you, never knowing what
might set him spinning, like a whirligig falling.

It all seems right: fingers intact and
wiggling, no obvious signs of trauma.
My worries for him are not
these small defeats and setbacks. I worry
that his dreams might fly out of his head,
circle above, out of reach like buzzards
over curvy county roads,
hawks over a henhouse.

So much loss on these roads, I think, and so
much that I am unable to fix.
The things I've lost I measure in
shadow, boxed inside my chest,
resting like flint.

Across his cheek, I smudge him,
pray to the god-of-small-boys,
more powerful than mother and
more present than I can be:
Carry my love like your best trinket
and follow the geese wherever they fly.

Solid, Grabbable

My dead have been coming
to me in my dreams. My father, in a stony
Greek landscape. Jennifer, still as the
last time I saw her, a plate of food
full in front of her. My old
dog, even. I have never been one to try
to see signs in dreams or in the sky—all
the places people say they see signs.
I don't hear anything in chimes but chimes,
no ghosts, no messages. And how sad
is that? Once, I was telling a story
about a dead relative and a lamp flickered.
It wasn't enough to convince me, though
my audience was wowed. I want to tell
my dead that if you come for me, really
come for me. Don't waste your energy
flickering lights. Can't you see that I want
you back here, solid, grabbable; that's what
I cry for. Anything else leaves
me emptier.

I Tell You About Sleeping Trees

When trees droop at night, they might actually be 'sleeping'
—Washington Post *headline, 20 May 2016*

David, when you were new
and I couldn't put you down

for all the crying you did
the way you grabbed at empty air

made me feel shelled
though I was only feet from you

I would sing you a song. *Not You Are
My Sunshine* or *Rock-a-bye Baby*

one that has this line:
        It's funny how my world goes round without you

I have always felt guilty about
singing that to you. Like those words

might fly too far into the universe and
I would have to try it—

to live without you.
On vacation, when we still traveled with

port-a-cribs and baby monitors,
I sang you to sleep with the Atlantic

keeping time outside the sliding
glass door. If all the world went

to sleep—all the trees, all the waves, all the birds—
but we did not, could breathe in all the slumber

the two of us: what secrets
would we learn? Standing

in the silence of the trees' canopy
maybe we could hear their lullaby.

After Death: An Inventory, Beginning With a Dog
with a line from Anne Sexton

The winter descends here, a few
yellow leaves hanging on. I am
walking down the street, our street,
with your dog. My dog now.
Small, a terrier, unlike the hunting dogs I
have always kept. She's wearing a coat.
This dog, I call her my imprinted
duckling. At my heels when I cook, at my hip
when I sit. She burrows under the down
of my blanket, and I wonder how
she breathes under there, her pushed-in nose
flush against the softness.

From your bedroom, from a mirrored tray
from the top of your dresser, I took
the half-full bottle of Chanel No. 5,
slipped it into my purse, felt like a thief.
There's no way not to feel like this, like a vulture,
scavenging for the thing that will help
keep you in my memory.
Horsehead bookends. A tiny bust of Plato
I bought for you in Greece. A pocket-
sized copy of *The Gift of the Magi*. Your pincushion.

The winter has descended, but the sycamore
disagrees, holds its crispy leaves tight.

I thought about your practicality, and took
a few perfectly folded bath towels. This morning
when I dried off, the dog sniffed at one, sat
at my feet, licked my ankles.

Let's Say

A beachball bouncing down the road
in the December wind. The clouds, round,
mammatus. White caps on the river.
These gray days, these short days, I drive
to work in the dark and back home in the dark.
On winter days like this, I miss Tucson. Not the
ex-lover I met there and then ran back East
to forget. I miss the bike, a Peugeot that I loved.
I'd ride to Time Market from my little place at
7th and Euclid for Marlboros. I miss Catalina
Park. Late night drunken burritos from Los Betos.
Sunsets that stretch the entire sky. In Tucson,
the time never changes. No fall back, spring forward.
My husband said to me yesterday that we
only have now. That I live in the past, always
wishing to change unchangeable things. So I change
them here, in this poem. Let's say I went home
with Tyson, not the ex-lover. When Paul crashed
his Vespa in front of my place, I didn't bake
him a loaf of bread. I let Carolyn kiss me and I kept
the dogs. In Tucson, the time never changes.
I am still 18, 19, 20, bad hair and bad decisions.
On winter days, it makes sense to me to miss the sun.

How I Spent My Day, Two Years After
My Father's Death

for Tom Rogowski

Morning, February, a bit brighter every
day. One boy, Cheerios, an argument
about sugar. The other, a poached egg.
Toast. Sleep-stumbling through the house in my bathrobe,
searching for matching socks, dumping laundry
baskets for clean shirts, the right pants
for each child. Brew coffee.

There is a picture of my father hanging
in my dining room. Montana, a window in a barn.
Stalk of wheat in his mouth. It is a recreation
of a photo taken 45 years ago. Save
for the wheat. 45 years ago it was a Marlboro.

Load the dishwasher to save the trouble
of doing it in the evening. I wonder
why I don't usually do this, but I know
why. I'm never this meticulous, this
focused in the almost-dark of almost-spring
mornings, or any mornings at all.

There is a picture of my father on my
living room bookshelf. It's a selfie he sent.
He's half-in, half-out of the frame. Napa, my brother's
courtyard. My mother, my brother, his girlfriend
waving. Tomato plants vine up the fence,
they have glasses of wine, fresh bruschetta.

Pull a hot bath. I'm at my mother's house.
She is with my brother in Texas. I have
wine. I have words rattling in the back
of my head. My small dog curls on the bathmat,
settles in for as long as I might take.

There is a picture of my father with my niece.
My father at my brother's wedding. A portrait
of my parents on a wedding anniversary. Caption:
Still crazy after 39 years. A photo of my mother
and father on her dresser, at my uncle's wedding. I've always
teased her that she had Marilyn Quayle hair.

Start supper, wine-stumbling in the kitchen
playlist stuck on "America":
    Alexa, play "America"
    again (empty and aching but I don't know why)
and I'll end the day the same way it started:
dumping the baskets, this time for pajamas.
Wondering what was out that Montana barn window.

Murmuration

It's like lightning in reverse, the starlings
rising from the shorn field.
Dark and moving in a confusing
undulating group
and I know from spellbinding YouTube
videos it's called a murmuration.
It seems anything but that beautiful word,
with their hum, the muttering, the rushing.
When I murmur in your ear
let's get out of here
and later we turn into a confusing undulating
tangle, I get it.
The perfectly uncoordinated coordination,
the sound of fire crackling between
us, unrecognizable shapes not
in the sky
but completely earthbound,
harmonious colliding,
unchoreographed choreography.

My Husband Sends Me Running From the Garden

Last summer, you were hammering
tomato stakes row after row
and I had to leave the garden to get
you cold water. It was the swinging
motion of your shoulders, the final
flex of the latissimus dorsi, the rippling
of the deltoid that sent me from the bed
of snap peas to the kitchen for relief.
For you, yes, but also for me.

When We Were Young

we bought things like violas without a second thought.

We had lost weekends in Nashville
or our tiki-ed out backyard, no regard

for hangovers. No need for baby
monitors. We wore bathing suits. My skin

did not need nightly Retinol.
When we were young I didn't feel

so dusty, so slow. Now, I am planning for
a hysterectomy. In bed, you say

things to me like, *You don't have to prop
your breasts up like that to make them appealing to me.*

There's no reason I shouldn't believe
you, but I don't. When I lie on my back

and my breasts slide down to my sides
leaving my chest flat,

I feel nothing but old. Laden.
It doesn't matter what my body has done,

it matters what it does not do anymore.

Your Mother Never Took Physics, David

You are staring out the window
at a barge cutting through the river
or maybe power lines when you ask me
Is white a color? I tell you it's all the colors
lined into one,
that white is light, and all the colors
are in the light and when we see a rainbow
the colors break out and
show themselves to us.

No idea how to explain things
like this to you. Explain light,
absence of light, white,
black *(I am begging you in my head*
not to ask about black, because
isn't black all the colors, too?) and all that stuff
we find between.
That in-between stuff.
What we, I hope, are mostly made of.

The Release

I am on the bank of the Pigeon River.
The woman upstream is fly-fishing.
I am trying to keep my smallish boys
in line, quiet, to not break
her concentration. I've never been a swimming
hole-type of woman, but this river has one,
swirls blue green in the sun
shards, almost lures me in past my ankles.
She casts and the lime green line floats close.
She casts and the line moves like a sound
wave, even whirrs before it splashes.
My Greek grandfather tied his own flies,
now lost to time and an estate sale.
I remember his back better than I remember
his face: flannel against the Michigan spring,
sitting at the end of his dock on Mona Lake.
I grabbed mussels from the shoreline, swatted
black flies, watched his large hands
bring the rod back, watched its arc, then
the release. I lose myself
to the kingfisher across the river, watch
him and his orange chest hunt from above.
And then she does it, almost without me noticing:
brings in the fish, river trout,
pink-bellied, sleek as a bullet, slips it into her creel.

The Same Situation

In my dream, we fought about Joni Mitchell,
you saying that Blue beats Court and Spark

by a mile, me holding up that pale peach album,
the sea stretching to embrace the mountains.

And maybe it does, I don't know.
But it was the unprompted undulation of my

body, after hearing those first muted guitar
chords of Help Me that sealed it when I was 15,

thieving my dad's records & laying belly-down
on the blue carpet of my suburban bedroom.

My dad played it at the Union at Ohio State,
over and over, he said, trying to follow her

chord changes, trying to follow her rhythms.
There's no following that, he told me.

Awake, you & I don't fight about Joni,
but about things less important: my dirty car,

the laundry I left in the basket on the stairs.
Nobody wants to hear about another's dreams,

but I will tell you anyway: the clouds hung low, &
a heron beat against a strong wind, flapping but unmoving.

Late April Aubade With Snow

with thanks to Cory Maillet

If it's going to snow in April,
then let them be the biggest snowflakes ever.

Let it happen in the earliest of the morning,
with coffee ready, and a few moments to spare
before the house wakes up.

Let the creaks of the floor boards guide you to the window.

Let the wonder of it take over the astonishment,
take over even the small jag of anger you feel as you survey the
covered garden, and hope that the small shoots will make it.

Remember that they will, small shoots find ways,
and think of the sunflower you saw on the news that
grew in a cracked highway that commuters slowed down to avoid.

If it is going to snow in April, remember it won't last.

Remember that soon the small of your back will be beaded with
sweat, and that your favorite season is all of them.

Forgotten Ohio

About this time, I start believing
that spring has forgotten Ohio.
I am dying for green, and then
remember that it is only mid-February.
Too early for all that birth, too early
for reclaiming the tips of the elms and
sycamores, shoots of the daffodils.
What if I gave up on everything
as easily as I have given up on green?
Like I gave up on jogging or learning
to recognize the call of the wood thrush
and the tufted tit mouse. I stand outside
like a sundial, greedily taking the warmth
from the sun, feeling guilty for the shade
of the brown grass in my shadow.

Appalachian Spring

I really feel it today, the way the hills are starting
to green up— from a distance the buds are celadon

lattice work, looking lacy on slopes that just a few
days ago I was sure were bare shoulders shrugging at me.
Yesterday was the part in Appalachian Spring where the

strings come blooming in and if the redbuds weren't already
bursting, those violins would convince them that it's time.

Between piccolo notes is a highwire that squirrels run.
Yesterday was the part with the robin bobbing on the
fence, looking at me cock-eyed with a twig in his beak.

Yesterday was the part where I roll down the windows,
where I welcome the pollen stain on the knees of my jeans.

Tomorrow we'll pick the violets for jelly, and I will
remember this day later, maybe in the dead heat of
July, when the grass starts to crisp up.

On Breaking and Mending

I remember every day that I know nothing.
I patch the holes at the knees and dress minor wounds.
There is no good place to sit and watch
the trees rattle in the wind,
so I ask you to run with a branch
like a kite behind you so I can hear that whoosh,
but mind the holes where the dog has dug
and watch the clothesline.

Everything is fragile, like mended china
and I fear bones might break like chalk.
There are lines where things have half-way healed
but nothing is as it was.
I am tired of fearing the coming of seasons
and preparing for emptiness.
The garden is empty. The henhouse is empty.
One day the car seats will be empty.
It that when we will ask each other
What have we done to ourselves?

I know nothing of yesterday's heartbreak.
It is replaced by what has happened today.
I try to remember that I am built of stars.
That every flash of a firefly is a miracle.
That my world can be bigger than the puddle
where the tadpoles wiggle circles.
Yet, I mind the rules.
I do not stray from this orbit.

Acknowledgments

My unending thanks goes to Dr. Ross Tangedal and the staff at Cornerstone Press for selecting my manuscript as part of the Portage Poetry Series. I also want to thank Kala Buttke for her guidance and help. I did not know what to expect from the editing process, and she was a perfect guide. Thank you for your kindness and for reading the work so closely.

Thank you to the women in my writing group: Courtney LeBlanc, Amy Haddad, Ashley Steineger, Chelsea Risley, and Caroline Earleywine. Each of you lift me up and make my work better.

Kelli Russell Agodon helped me when all I could see was failure. Thank you, thank you.

Thank you also to the poets I was privileged to work with while at Queens University of Charlotte: Ada Limón, Morri Creech, Robert Polito, and Cathy Smith-Bowers.

Special gratitude also to Maggie Smith, a good friend and inspiration for many years, and hopefully many more. You answer my dumb questions and make me Dutch babies, and I love you much.

Without the support of my family, this book wouldn't exist. My earliest reader and sounding board, my husband and partner John, who always has my back and who writes better than I do. My brothers, who put up with my weirdness and love me anyway. My Aunt Jill, who started letting me borrow books when I was small. And my mother, Candace, my best friend.

I love and thank you all.

* * *

Gratefully acknowledged are the journals and publications in which particular poems first appeared:

"Justin Timberlake Sings During My First Mammogram", published in *Glass Poetry*; "When We Were Young", first published in *Ghost City Press*; "Thursday Morning, Early, With Fog", first published in *Literary Mama*; "Naked In the Macy's Changing Room, Trying to Think About Anything Other Than the Election", first published in *Split This Rock*; "Intervention For the Intervention Specialist", "Poem In Which My Body Calls Me a Bitch", "I Speak to My Husband From Inside a Whale", "Stockholm", first published in *Dodging the Rain*; "My Dog Lifted His Leg", first published in *8Poems*; "Burying the Draft Mare In February", first published in *Bird's Thumb*; "Safeguards", first published in *Jarfly*; "Laundry List", first published in *MORIA*; "Naming", first published in *Oyez Review*; "Scene From a Yellow Kitchen", first published in *The Pikeville Review*; "Small Town Haibun", first published in *Riggwelter*; "The Doe", first published in *District Lit*; "First Inclinations", first published in *Calamus*; "Whirligig", first published in *Four Ties Lit Review*; "Walking Past Abandoned Houses, I Think of Eric", first published in *Not Far From Me: Stories of Opioids and Ohio* (Ohio State University Press); "After I Tell You About Sleeping Tress", "David Defines Infinity", first published in *Mothers Always Write*; "After Death: An Inventory", "Yesterday I Asked My Son", "Circa 1994", first published in *Appalachian Review*; "Let's Say", first published in *Sheila-Na-Gig*; "Discernable Proof", "Trillium as Accomplishment", first published in *Northern Appalachia Review*.

BARBARA COSTAS-BIGGS is a poet and librarian from Southern Ohio. Her work has appeared in *Appalachian Review*, *Northern Appalachian Review*, *The Pikeville Review*, *8Poems*, and others. Her chapbook, *The Other Shore*, was a finalist for the Washburn Prize from *Harbor Review*. She holds an MFA from Queens University of Charlotte and an MLIS from Kent State University.

CPSIA information can be obtained
at www.ICGtesting.com
Printed in the USA
LVHW092306120222
711010LV00004B/199